DK EYEWITNESS WORKBOOKS
Ancient Egypt

by Jen Green

Penguin
Random
House

Editorial Consultant Charlotte Booth
Educational Consultants Linda B. Gambrell
and Geraldine Taylor

Senior Editors Rob Houston, Ankush Saikia, Fleur Star
Senior Art Editor Sarah Ponder
Editor Anuroop Sanwalia
US Editor Jennette ElNaggar
Art Editor Mahua Mandal, Tanisha Mandal
DTP Designer Dheeraj Arora, Anita Yadav
DK Picture Library Claire Bowers, Romaine Werblow
Managing Editors Christine Stroyan, Shikha Kulkarni
Managing Art Editors Anna Hall, Govind Mittal
Production Editor Tom Morse
Production Controller Rachel Ng
Senior Jacket Designer Suhita Dharamjit
Jacket Design Development Manager Sophia MTT
Publisher Andrew Macintyre
Art Director Karen Self
Publishing Director Jonathan Metcalf

This American Edition, 2020
First American Edition, 2008
Published in the United States by DK Publishing
1450 Broadway, Suite 801, New York, NY 10018

Copyright © 2008, 2020 Dorling Kindersley Limited
DK, a Division of Penguin Random House LLC
20 21 22 23 24 10 9 8 7 6 5 4 3 2 1
001–323000–Jun/2020

A catalog record for this book
is available from the Library of Congress.
ISBN 978-0-7440-3448-6

DK books are available at special discounts when purchased in bulk
for sales, promotions, premiums, fund-raising, or educational use.
For details, contact: DK Publishing Special Markets,
1450 Broadway, Suite 801, New York, NY 10018.
SpecialSales@dk.com

Printed and bound in Canada.

For the curious

www.dk.com

Contents

Fast Facts

How This Book Can Help Your Child

Eyewitness Workbooks offer a fun and colorful range of stimulating titles on the subjects of history, science, and geography. Devised and written with the expert advice of educational consultants, each workbook aims to:

- develop a child's knowledge of a popular topic
- provide practice of key skills and reinforce classroom learning
- nurture a child's special interest in a subject

About this book

Eyewitness Workbooks Ancient Egypt is an activity-packed guide to the history of a fascinating civilization. Inside you will find:

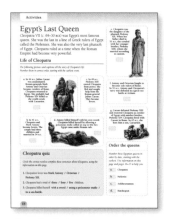

Fast Facts

This section presents key information as concise facts that are easy to digest, learn, and remember. Encourage your child to start by reading through the valuable information in the Fast Facts section and studying the statistics charts at the back of the book before trying out the activities.

Activities

The enjoyable, fill-in activities are designed to develop information recall and help your child practice cross-referencing skills. Each activity can be completed using information provided on the page, in the Fast Facts section, or on the charts at the back of the book.

Quick Quiz

There are six pages of multiple-choice questions to test your child's newfound knowledge of the subject. Children should try answering the quiz questions only once all of the Activity section has been completed.

Important information

- The recipe on page 35 uses nuts, dates, and honey. This activity should be avoided by anyone with an allergy to any of these foods. It also involves using a knife, which an adult should supervise. All other activities can be carried out by children without adult supervision.

- Some children may require assistance for the drawing activity on page 33 and the bracelet activity on page 34.

- Encourage your child's interest with a museum visit to see Egyptian exhibits, or with further research online and at your local library.

PROGRESS CHART

Chart your progress as you work through the activity and quiz pages in this book.
First check your answers, then color in a star in the correct box below.

Page	Topic	Star	Page	Topic	Star	Page	Topic	Star
14	Farming along the Nile	☆	24	Everlasting Bodies	☆	34	Fashion and Makeup	☆
15	The Pharaohs' Rule	☆	25	Mummy's Case	☆	35	Food and Feasts	★
16	A Boy Pharaoh	☆	26	Pharaohs' Funerals	★	36	Markets and Trade	☆
17	Famous Kings and Queens	☆	27	Journey to the Afterlife	☆	37	Living on the Nile	☆
18	Egypt's Last Queen	★	28	The First Pyramids	☆	38	The Pharaohs	☆
19	Gods and Goddesses	☆	29	Later Pyramids	★	39	Religion	☆
20	Magic and Medicine	☆	30	Pyramid Building	★	40	Mummification and the Afterlife	☆
21	Scribes and Sculptors	☆	31	Valley of the Kings	☆	41	Pyramids	☆
22	Hieroglyphs	★	32	War and Weapons	★	42	Writing, Arts, and Crafts	☆
23	Temples and Priests	☆	33	Painting and Portraits	★	43	Daily Life	☆

Ancient Egypt

More than 5,000 years ago, one of the world's oldest and greatest civilizations developed in Egypt in north Africa. Egypt's prosperity was based on the Nile River, which made farming possible. The Egyptians invented a system of writing and became great scholars and artists. Ancient Egypt is famous for its magnificent temples and tombs.

The Nile

The Greek scholar Herodotus called Egypt "the gift of the Nile." The river watered the strip of land along its banks, transforming desert into green fields. The Nile also acted as a watery highway and provided food such as fish.

Pyramids of Giza
Memphis

Nile Delta

Nile River

Valley of the Kings   Luxor

The land of Egypt

Key facts

- Every year, the Nile flooded, depositing rich mud that made the land fertile.
- Farmers raised river water with a device called a shadoof. They dug ditches to channel the water through their fields of crops.
- The Nile provided the main mode of transportation in ancient Egypt. People traveled in boats made of reeds or wood.

Early history

By 3200 BCE, two kingdoms had grown up along the Nile: Upper Egypt in the south, and Lower Egypt in the north. In 3100 BCE, King Narmer united the two. Egyptian history is divided into three main periods, called the Old, Middle, and New Kingdoms. In between were times of unrest.

Key facts

- Early Dynastic Period (c. 3100–2686 BCE). This era began when King Narmer united Egypt.
- Old Kingdom (c. 2686–2181 BCE). A period of strong rule and the great age of pyramid building.
- First Intermediate Period (c. 2181–2055 BCE). A time of great unrest.
- Middle Kingdom (c. 2055–1650 BCE). An age of powerful kings who ruled from the city of Thebes.

King Djoser of the Old Kingdom

Later history

Tutankhamun ruled briefly in New Kingdom times

At its height, the Egyptian Empire stretched from Nubia in the south all the way to modern Iraq. However, after 747 BCE, Egypt was often ruled by foreign empires. In 30 BCE, it was conquered by Rome.

Key facts

- Second Intermediate Period (c. 1650–1550 BCE). A time of unrest, when Egypt was conquered by the Hyksos.
- New Kingdom (c. 1550–1069 BCE). The Hyksos were driven out, and Egypt became powerful again.
- Third Intermediate Period (c. 1069–747 BCE). A period of unrest, invasion, and foreign rule.
- Late period (c. 747–332 BCE). Persia ruled Egypt for part of this.
- Ptolemaic Period (c. 332–30 BCE). Greek leader Alexander the Great conquered Egypt in 332 BCE. His general Ptolemy founded the Ptolemaic dynasty. In 30 BCE, Egypt became part of the Roman Empire.

Pharaohs

Egypt was ruled by powerful kings, known as pharaohs. On the king's death, the throne passed to his son, forming ruling families called dynasties. Various dynasties ruled from different capitals, including Memphis (near modern Cairo) and later Thebes (modern Luxor).

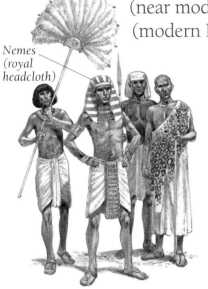

Nemes (royal headcloth)

A pharaoh attended by his fan bearer

Royal power

The Egyptian pharaohs held all the highest offices in the land: chief priest, head judge, and commander in chief of the army. The pharaoh was believed to be descended from the sun god Re. The god Horus spoke through him. The pharaoh was a link between the gods and the people.

Key facts

- The title pharaoh comes from *per-Aa*, which meant "Great House." It was a mark of great respect.
- The pharaoh ruled through one or two chief ministers called viziers, who headed the administrators who ran the kingdom.
- In later times, Egyptian kings led their armies into battle.

Famous queens

Pharaohs often married their sister or half sister to keep the royal bloodline pure. Egyptian queens rarely held power in their own right. They usually held only the title of "great royal wife." However, a few queens became powerful.

Key facts

- Hatshepsut (ruled 1473–1458 BCE) was one of Egypt's greatest queens. When her husband, Tuthmosis II, died, she ruled for her young son.
- Nefertiti (*c.* 1370–1330 BCE) was the wife of Akhenaten, who transformed the Egyptian religion. She may have coruled with her husband.
- Cleopatra (*c.* 69–30 BCE) was the last Ptolemaic ruler. She ruled with her Roman husband, Mark Antony, but in 31 BCE, they were defeated by Rome.

Part of a statue of Cleopatra

Great pharaohs

In the course of its 3,000-year history, Egypt had many great kings who built mighty empires. Their magnificent tombs record their victories. The pharaoh wore a double crown that symbolized the two kingdoms that had been united by King Narmer.

Crown of Upper Egypt

A pharaoh of Upper Egypt

Key facts

- Tuthmosis III (1479–1425 BCE) was a great commander. Under his strong leadership, Egypt won a large empire.
- Akhenaten (1353–1336 BCE) was originally known as Amenhotep IV. He reformed Egypt's religion, worshipping only the sun god Aten.
- Tutankhamun, Akhenaten's son, became king at the age of nine. In his brief reign (1333–1323 BCE), Egypt's old religion was restored.
- Ramses II (*c.* 1279–1213 BCE) ruled Egypt for 67 years. He commissioned many fine buildings, including the temples at Abu Simbel and Nubia.

Egyptian Society

Egyptian society was shaped like a pyramid, with the pharaoh at the top, and nobles, priests, and overseers making an upper class below him. Craftspeople and traders formed a middle layer, with farmers and laborers at the base. People could improve their position in society if their business prospered or if they married well.

Upper classes

Well-to-do people included noble families, landowners, chief priests, and head scribes. There were also high-ranking officials and army officers. Key positions in the government were often held by members of the royal family.

Key facts

• Wealthy families lived in fine town houses with two stories. Some rich people had country villas with as many as 70 rooms, including servants' quarters.

• Rich people held banquets to entertain friends and celebrate festivals. Roasted meats, cakes, figs, and wine were served.

• The sons of noblemen were sometimes educated by scribes. Daughters did not receive formal schooling but were taught at home.

A nobleman

Middle classes

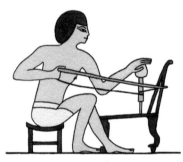

A carpenter

The middle tier was made up of skilled workers such as craftsmen, merchants, and lower-ranking officials. Middle-class people had one- or two-story homes with several rooms. The sons of craftsmen usually followed their father's trade.

Key facts

• Craftsmen included masons, carpenters, smiths, cloth makers, leatherworkers, and boatbuilders. Women did spinning and weaving.

• The finest craftsmen worked on royal tombs. Using valuable minerals, gemstones, and hardwoods, they made sculptures, jewelry, and fine furniture.

• Lower-ranking officials ran the local government and collected taxes. For the purposes of control, Egypt was divided into 42 districts called nomes.

Ordinary people

Most people were farmers, laborers, and servants. There were also some enslaved people who had usually been captured in battle. In the late period, enslaved people signed a contract with their masters and had some rights. Townspeople lived in small, flat-roofed houses on narrow streets.

Farmers harvesting wheat

Key facts

• Farmers grew crops such as wheat and barley, and reared animals such as cattle, sheep, and pigs. Oxen were used to pull plows.

• Every year, farmers paid part of their crop to the king as tax. They also gave their labor to help build public works such as pyramids and other royal tombs.

• Poor houses had few rooms. Flat roofs were used for storage and cooking, and people slept there when it was hot.

A brickmaker at work

Religion

The Egyptians were very religious. They worshipped hundreds of different gods who looked after various parts of daily life. Many gods and goddesses were closely related. For example, Osiris, god of the dead, was married to his sister Isis. People prayed to particular gods to survive difficult times.

Temples

Temple of the goddess Isis

Temples were the gods' homes on Earth. At the heart of these impressive buildings was an inner shrine, which held a gold statue of the god. Only priests, priestesses, and the pharaoh were allowed to enter the temple.

Key facts

- Temples and also royal tombs were built of stone because they were built to last forever. Other buildings, even palaces, were made of mud bricks.
- People visited temples on religious festivals, which were celebrated with prayers, processions, feasting, and dancing. But they were not allowed inside.
- People usually prayed at home, at a little altar in the house. Some people had a chapel in the garden.

Priests

High-ranking priests were rich and powerful. Their main role was to take care of the gods and stand in for the pharaoh by presiding at ceremonies. The position of high priest often passed from father to son and was held by generations of the same family until a pharaoh appointed an outsider.

Key facts

- High priests commanded the wealth of temple treasuries. Temples owned extensive lands.
- Lower orders of priests conducted minor ceremonies and tended the gods' statues. They also looked after temple property and kept records.
- Statues of the gods were brought out of the sanctuary every day. They were washed, dressed, and offered food that had been purified with holy water.

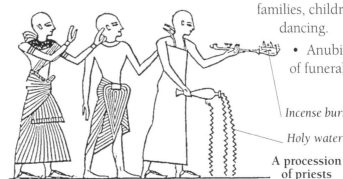

Incense burner

Holy water

A procession of priests

Gods and goddesses

Each village, town, and district had its own gods. The main gods were worshipped at national festivals. Many gods were shown with the heads of animals who represented their personality. This made them easy to identify.

Falcon-headed Horus, god of the sky

Key facts

- Re, the sun god, was the main god of the Old and Middle Kingdom. He became Amun-Re, king of the gods, in New Kingdom times.
- Thoth, god of wisdom, gave the Egyptians writing, mathematics, and medicine.
- Osiris was Lord of the underworld and the afterlife.
- The goddess Isis was the wife and sister of Osiris.
- Horus, the sky god, looked after the pharaoh.
- Bes, the dwarf god, looked after families, children, and also dancing.
- Anubis was the god of funerals and embalming.

Death and the Afterlife

The Egyptians believed in an afterlife, or life beyond death. The spirits of the dead were thought to journey to an underworld called Duat, where they would be tested. But to live forever, the body had to be preserved. This led the Egyptians to perfect the art of mummification.

Funeral rites

A funeral barge carrying the pharaoh's mummified body

Mummies

A mummy is a body that has been preserved with the skin intact. The Egyptians became so skilled at mummification that some 5,000-year-old bodies are still well preserved today. There were several degrees of mummification, depending on how much the family could afford.

Key facts

- The first stage of mummification was to remove certain organs, which were preserved in special jars. The body was packed in natron salt to dry it. Then it was wrapped in linen strips and placed in a coffin.
- Mummification took up to 70 days. The drying process took 40 days.
- Before burial, people believed the mummy was brought to life by the Opening of the Mouth ritual.

The afterlife

The Egyptians believed death was a temporary stage on the journey to everlasting life. If found worthy, the spirits of the dead would live forever in the Kingdom of the West. But first they had to pass a trial, which judged whether they had lived a good life.

Protective amulet worn by the dead

Key facts

- People who had lived a good life went to a land that was like Egypt, but without hardship.
- Prayers were said during mummification to protect the spirit and help it reach the afterlife.

Wealthy Egyptians were buried with elaborate rituals, including prayers, processions, and displays of grief by hired mourners. Funerals of pharaohs were very elaborate. Ordinary people also had prayers and processions, but on a much smaller scale.

Key facts

- People were buried with possessions that would help them in the afterlife. These included food, drink, clothes, and sometimes even furniture.
- Wealthy people were buried with magical statues of servants, called shabti. If the dead person was ordered to work in the afterlife, the shabti would do it for them.
- The Egyptians buried their dead in the western desert. This place, where the sun set, was the land of the dead.
- Pharaohs were buried after 70 days of public mourning, during which the body was mummified. The mummy in its coffin was carried up the Nile to the tomb.
- The pharaoh was believed to join the sun god and sail across the sky daily in a sacred boat.

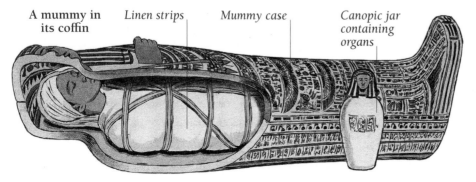

A mummy in its coffin   *Linen strips*   *Mummy case*   *Canopic jar containing organs*

The Pyramids

The Egyptians were skillful architects and master builders. They built magnificent pyramids as tombs for their pharaohs. These enormous monuments housed the king's body and treasures for the afterlife. Some queens were buried in smaller pyramids. Egypt has more than 100 pyramids, all built west of the Nile.

Early pyramids

The Step Pyramid

The age of pyramid building lasted from about 2650 to 1650 BCE. The first pyramids had stepped sides. They were designed as gigantic stairways, which the pharaoh's soul would use to climb to heaven. Later pyramids had straight sides.

Key facts

- The first pyramid was built for King Djoser in about 2650 BCE by his architect Imhotep. Called the Step Pyramid, it rises in six tiers.
- The first pyramids with straight sides were built by King Sneferu around 2550 BCE. The first example was built at Meidum.
- Sneferu's second pyramid, the Bent Pyramid, has sides that change angle partway up. Sneferu's third pyramid has an even shape.

Pyramids of Giza

The pyramids of Giza are the finest Egyptian pyramids. They were built about 4,500 years ago as tombs for three Old Kingdom pharaohs: Khufu, Khafre, and Menkaure. They stand in the desert west of Memphis and are guarded by a stone sphinx.

Key facts

- The Great Pyramid rose to 482 ft (147 m) high. It is the tomb of Khufu, and it took 20 years to build.
- The Great Pyramid's sides were built to face exactly north, south, east, and west.
- The Sphinx has a body of a lion, but its features are thought to be a portrait of King Khafre.

The Sphinx guarding the pyramids of Giza

Pyramid building

The pyramids were built not by enslaved people but by ordinary Egyptians, working for the king as a kind of annual national service. These monuments are amazing feats of construction. The huge stones were cut from local quarries and hauled to the site using sledges and ropes.

Climbing the pyramids is illegal today

The Great Pyramid's immense blocks dwarf these 19th-century visitors

Key facts

- Huge numbers of ordinary Egyptians joined the pyramid workforce for three months every year. This was during the Nile flood, when no work could be done in the fields.
- The huge stones were hauled up sloping ramps, which rose higher as construction progressed.
- The great age of pyramid building was during the Old Kingdom.
- During the Middle Kingdom, more pyramids were built, using mud bricks and faced with stone.

11

Everyday Life

Egyptian families were quite large, with many children. Death in childhood was common, so parents needed many children to carry on their work. People wore light clothing, which was suited to the hot climate. Most people ate a healthy diet.

Families

A noble family talk while seated on finely carved chairs

The father was head of the household in ancient Egypt. The oldest son was his heir. However, women were well respected and had certain rights. They could own property and do business. Pharaohs often had several wives.

Key facts

- Girls might marry at the age of 12, boys at 14–15. Girls stayed at home until they married.
- Egyptian homes did not have much furniture. Better-off people sat on chairs or stools, and there were also chests, beds, and low tables.
- In poor families, children as young as seven had to work.

Clothing and beauty

Light, cool clothing was essential in Egypt's hot climate. Men wore kilts, and women wore simple tunics or dresses with shoulder straps. In later years, pleats became fashionable. Cloaks were worn in cool weather. Children are usually shown wearing nothing but jewelry.

Key facts

- Wealthy people wore clothes made of fine linen. Poorer people's clothes were of coarser linen.
- Men and women often shaved their heads. Wealthy people wore wigs. Children also had shaved heads, with one or more long locks of hair.
- Men and women wore makeup, especially dark eyeliner. Women also painted their lips and nails.

A well-off lady is refreshed by her attendants

Food and drink

Grape treaders　*Grape juice*　*Amphorae (vessels)*

Treading grapes to make wine

Egyptians generally ate a balanced diet with vegetables such as onions, leeks, and lettuce. The staple food was bread, made from wheat. People also ate pulses such as beans and lentils, along with fish, eggs, meat, and dairy products. However, poor people did not eat much meat.

Figs were also used to make wine

Key facts

- The main drink was beer, brewed from barley. Wine was also made, from grapes, figs, or dates.
- Grain to make flour was stored in granaries to keep it fresh. As well as bread, bakers made cakes. Honey was used to sweeten cakes and other food.
- People ate using their fingers. In wealthy households, a servant brought water to wash between courses.

Work and Play

Most Egyptians had to work hard to feed their families, with little time for leisure. However, there are several written reports of strikes and complaints about lazy workers. Some wealthy people lived a life of luxury without having to work.

Trade and barter

Egypt was one of the richest countries in the ancient world. Its wealth was based on farming and also valuable minerals, such as gold and copper. Egyptians did not use money. Instead, they exchanged goods and services for other produce or work of equal value. This practice is known as barter.

Gold mined east of the Nile was used in trade

Key facts

- Goods were valued according to a standard weight of copper called a deben. For example, a goat worth 4 deben might be traded for 4 deben worth of grain.
- Egypt developed trade links with neighboring nations, including lands on the shores of the Mediterranean and Red seas.
- Egyptian traders exchanged crops, minerals, papyrus, and wine for luxury goods such as wood, horses, and leopard skins from lands such as Syria to the northeast and Nubia to the south.

Scribes and writing

A scribe

Around 3300 BCE, the Egyptians invented a form of picture writing called hieroglyphics. Trained writers, known as scribes, were important people. They kept records for temples and for government departments and wrote letters for ordinary people who couldn't read or write.

Key facts

- Egyptian hieroglyphics used hundreds of different symbols. The writing could be read from left to right, right to left, or top to bottom.
- Hieroglyphs were used to write important texts such as temple inscriptions. For everyday life, a simpler script called hieratic was often used. Later, scribes invented an even simpler, faster script, called demotic.
- Egyptians wrote on paper called papyrus, made from Nile reeds.

Leisure time

There were no official holidays in ancient Egypt. However people did not work on religious festivals. In later times, these took up a third of the year, so some people took a lot of time off. Children and adults enjoyed sports such as sailing, gymnastics, and fishing. Board games and storytelling were also popular.

A musical instrument called a sistrum (rattle)

Key facts

- Young children played with dolls, spinning tops, and wooden toys. They also played ball games, leapfrog, and knucklebones.
- A board game called senet was similar to backgammon, with moves determined by a throw of the dice.
- Noblemen enjoyed hunting waterfowl, gazelle, and even lions and hippos.
- Music, singing, and dancing provided entertainment at festivals and banquets.

A queen playing a game similar to chess

Farming along the Nile

Egypt's prosperity was based on farming. But the climate was hot and dry. Without the Nile, Egypt would have been a desert. The river's annual flood spread rich dark silt across the fields. This allowed farmers to grow crops such as wheat, barley, and flax. The farming year began with the flood.

Complete the farming calendar

Match the three seasons of the farming year with their descriptions. Use the information on this page to help you.

Growing season   Inundation   Harvest

1.....................................
The time of flood when no farming work was done.

2.....................................
Crops were sown at this time, then sprouted and ripened over winter.

3.....................................
Ripe crops were cut in spring. The grain was then threshed and winnowed.

Ripening wheat

Farmers sowed their crops in fields plowed by oxen.

Farming facts

- The farming year was divided into three seasons: the flood or inundation, the growing season, and the harvest.
- The floods lasted from June to September. No farm work could be done. Farmers helped build the pyramids and tended their animals.
- When the floods went down in October, farmers plowed their fields using oxen. Crops such as wheat were sown and then ripened until February. A device called a shadoof raised river water to irrigate crops.
- Crops were harvested from March to May, before the floods returned. Farmers cut the crop using sickles.
- Farmers drove their cattle over the cut crop to separate the grain from the stalks. This is called threshing.
- The grain was then tossed in the air so that the husks blew away. This is called winnowing. The processed grain was stored in granaries.

Did you know?

The Nile's annual flood was caused by heavy rain and snowmelt in the mountains far to the south, where the river rose.

Color the map

The annual flood deposited fertile black mud. The Egyptians called the narrow strip of land watered by the Nile Kemet ("the Black Land"). The barren land on either side was called Deshret ("the Red Land").

Color in the map using black for the flooded area and red for the desert. The map on page 6 will help you.

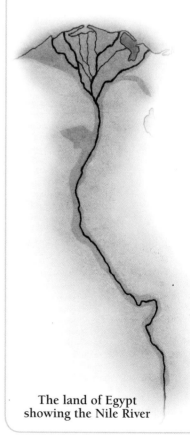

The land of Egypt showing the Nile River

The Pharaohs' Rule

For much of Egypt's history, pharaohs were thought to be living gods. The pharaoh had many responsibilities. He made offerings to the gods to ensure the annual flooding of the Nile. He maintained law and order and built temples and other monuments. In times of war, he led his soldiers into battle.

Complete the social pyramid

Egyptian society was arranged according to a strict hierarchy, in which some classes of people were considered more important and had more power than others.

Draw lines to link the descriptions of the classes with the tiers shown in the illustration. Use the information on page 8 to help you.

A pharaoh with some of his many servants

The upper class contained nobles, priests, officials, and scribes.

The pharaoh was all powerful.

Skilled craftworkers such as sculptors belonged to the middle class.

Unskilled workers such as farmers formed the lowest class.

Symbols of rule

Egyptian pharaohs wore several types of crowns. They also carried royal symbols called regalia to mark their high office.

Read the descriptions of the pharaohs' regalia and match the correct picture to its caption.

a.

1. The double crown combined the white crown of Upper Egypt (the valley) with the red crown of Lower Egypt (the delta).

b.

2. The blue crown was worn by pharaohs of New Kingdom times.

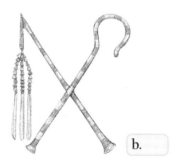

3. The striped royal headdress was called the nemes cloth.

c.

4. The shepherd's crook and flail for threshing wheat were symbols of kingship.

d.

15

A Boy Pharaoh

Tutankhamun came to the throne as a young boy and reigned for only a short time. He is famous because, in 1922, an archaeologist discovered his tomb complete with fabulous treasure. The tombs of all other pharaohs had been robbed of their treasures in ancient times.

Tutankhamun family quiz

Tutankhamun was probably the son of Akhenaten, the pharaoh who reformed Egypt's religion. Akhenaten had two wives: Queen Nefertiti, who bore him a daughter, and Kiya, who bore Tutankhamun. Tutankhamun married his half sister Ankhesenamun.

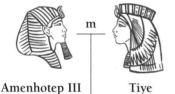

Amenhotep III
1390–1353 BCE

Tiye

Check all the statements that are true.

1. Tutankhamun had six half sisters.
2. Tutankhamun's mother was named Nefertiti.
3. Amenhotep III was Tutankhamun's uncle.
4. Queen Tiye was Akhenaten's mother.

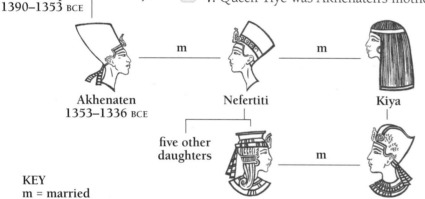

Akhenaten
1353–1336 BCE

Nefertiti

Kiya

five other daughters

Ankhesenamun

Tutankhamun
1333–1323 BCE

KEY
m = married
dates = pharaoh's reign, not life

Did you know?

Tutankhamun's father, Akhenaten, worshipped Aten, the sun disk, and banished all other gods.

Tutankhamun facts

- Tutankhamun was crowned in 1333 BCE at just nine years of age.
- Tutankhamun married his half sister soon after being crowned.
- Because he was still a boy, Tutankhamun was guided by his chief minister, Ay.
- Ay may have influenced Tutankhamun's decision to restore the old gods who had been banned by his father, Akhenaten.
- Tutankhamun died suddenly in 1323 BCE. Some experts believe he was murdered by Ay, who then seized the throne and married Ankhesenamun.

Tutankhamun's life story

The main events of Tutankhamun's history have been jumbled below. Put them in the right order by matching each description to the correct picture. Use the information on this page to help.

1.

2.

3.

4.

5.

a. Chief minister Ay instructs the boy king in his duties.

b. Tutankhamun dies in the ninth year of his reign.

c. The young Tutankhamun is crowned king.

d. Tutankhamun restores the old religion.

e. Tutankhamun marries his half sister Ankhesenamun.

Famous Kings and Queens

Ramses II and Khufu are famous because they commissioned magnificent buildings. Pharaohs often had several wives but only one queen. If the king had no sons, the throne could pass to his eldest daughter. Queen Hatshepsut was pharaoh in New Kingdom times.

Pharaoh facts

- Pepy II (2278–2184 BCE) became pharaoh when he was just six years old. His 94-year reign was the longest of all.

- Tuthmosis III (1479–1425 BCE) was short, just 5 ft (1.5 m), but a mighty warrior. His kingdom stretched as far as modern Iraq.

- Queen Hatshepsut (1473–1458 BCE) sent a fleet of ships to the land of Punt near Africa's east coast. When her husband died, she ruled for her stepson, Tuthmosis III, for 15 years.

- Tuthmosis IV (1400–1390 BCE) uncovered the statue of the Sphinx at Giza, which had been buried by sand.

Who is who?

Match the pharaohs with the descriptions of their reigns. Use the information on this page, on the chart at the back of the book, and on page 7 to help you.

Tuthmosis III   Ramses II   Khufu   Hatshepsut

1. This king commissioned the temples of Abu Simbel in Nubia ....
2. This small but warlike pharaoh carved out a great empire ....
3. This pharaoh sent an expedition to the mysterious land of Punt ....
4. This king built the Great Pyramid at Giza ....

A pharaoh dictates laws, which are recorded by scribes

Hatshepsut's family tree

Fill in Queen Hatshepsut's family tree using the information on this page. See Tutankhamun's family tree on page 16 as a guide to how the tree works.

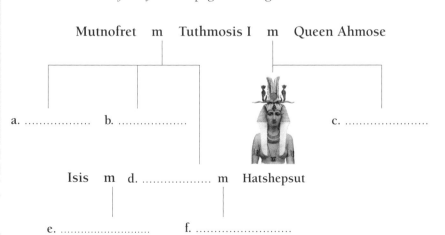

Mutnofret   m   Tuthmosis I   m   Queen Ahmose

a. ....   b. ....   c. ....

Isis   m   d. ....   m   Hatshepsut

e. ....   f. ....

Hatshepsut facts

- Hatshepsut was the daughter of Tuthmosis I and Queen Ahmose. Her younger sister Akhbetneferu died as a child.

- Tuthmosis I had a lesser wife, Mutnofret, who bore three sons: Wadjmose, Amenose, and Tuthmosis II.

- Hatshepsut married her half brother Tuthmosis II. The couple ruled Egypt and had a daughter, Neferure.

- Tuthmosis II also had a lesser wife, Isis, who bore a son, Tuthmosis III.

Egypt's Last Queen

Cleopatra VII (c. 69–30 BCE) was Egypt's most famous queen. She was the last in a line of Greek rulers of Egypt called the Ptolemies. She was also the very last pharaoh of Egypt. Cleopatra ruled at a time when the Roman Empire had become very powerful.

Life of Cleopatra

The following pictures and captions tell the story of Cleopatra's life. Number them in correct order, starting with the earliest event.

a. In 44 BCE, Julius Caesar was assassinated. Roman generals Mark Antony and Octavian became corulers of Rome. Cleopatra returned to Egypt. She probably had Ptolemy XIV killed so she could corule with Caesarion.

c. In 49 BCE, Ptolemy XIII ousted Cleopatra from power. She fled and sought help from the Roman general Julius Caesar. They became lovers.

b. In 41 BCE, Cleopatra and Mark Antony became lovers. The couple had three children and married in 34 BCE.

d. Antony killed himself with his own sword. Cleopatra killed herself by allowing a poisonous snake called an asp to bite her. Egypt came under Roman rule.

e. Cleopatra was the daughter of the pharaoh Ptolemy XII. When her father died in 51 BCE, she coruled with her younger brother, Ptolemy XIII, whom she married according to custom.

f. Antony and Octavian fought to become sole rulers of Rome. In 31 BCE, Antony and Cleopatra's navy was defeated in a great sea battle at Actium.

g. Caesar defeated Ptolemy XIII and restored Cleopatra as coruler of Egypt with another brother, Ptolemy XIV. Cleopatra lived with Caesar in Rome. In 47 BCE, she bore him a son, Caesarion.

Cleopatra quiz

Circle the correct word to complete these sentences about Cleopatra, using the information on this page.

1. Cleopatra's lover was **Mark Antony** / **Octavian** / **Ptolemy XII.**

2. Cleopatra had a total of **three** / **four** / **five** children.

3. Cleopatra killed herself **with a sword** / **using a poisonous snake** / **in a sea battle.**

Order the queens

Number these Egyptian queens in order by date, starting with the earliest. Use information on this page and pages 16–17 to help you.

a. Cleopatra

b. Nefertiti

c. Ankhesenamun

d. Hatshepsut

Gods and Goddesses

Hundreds of gods and goddesses were worshipped in ancient Egypt. Some were local, and others were known throughout the land. Some were patrons (guardians) of professions, such as medicine or writing. Many gods were represented by an animal that symbolized their powers.

Whose symbol?

Match these animals with their god and goddess. Use information on this page and on page 48 to help you.

Scarab beetle

Ibis

Ram

....

....

....

Cow

Cat

Jackal

....

....

....

Did you know?

Hathor, goddess of love, fertility, and childbirth, was shown as a cow or with cow's horns.

Hathor

Gods facts

- Thoth, patron god of scribes, was shown with the head of a bird called an ibis.
- Horus, the sky god, was shown with the head of a falcon.
- Ptah of Memphis was the patron of doctors and healers. His symbol was a sacred pillar.
- Khepri, god of renewal, rolled the sun disk across the sky. His symbol was a scarab beetle rolling a ball of dung.
- The goddess Bastet helped crops ripen. Her symbol was a cat.
- Sekhmet, goddess of war, was shown with the head of a lioness.

Who would you pray to?

Decide which god or goddess you would ask for help in the following areas if you lived in ancient Egypt. The information on this page will help you. Who would you pray to if ...

1. you were a soldier on the eve of battle. ....

2. you were a doctor about to attend to the pharaoh. ....

3. you were a young man training to be a scribe. ....

4. you were a wife about to give birth. ....

5. you were a farmer preparing for the harvest. ....

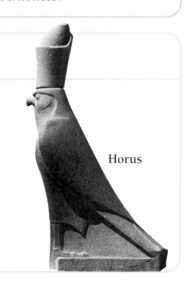

Horus

Magic and Medicine

Egyptian medicine was amazingly advanced for its time. Doctors had a good knowledge of anatomy and devised effective treatments for some illnesses. Certain plants were used in medicine. The Egyptians also looked to magic to cure illness and ward off evil. Some plants were thought to have magical properties. People wore charms called amulets to protect them from danger or evil.

Did you know?

The Egyptians used garlic in burial ceremonies. It was thought to provide protection against snakebites. Garlic was also used to get rid of tapeworms.

Select the magic plants

Use the information on this page to check the small boxes below. Check only the plants that were believed to have magic properties or were used in rituals.

Plant facts

- The juice of juniper berries was used in rituals to purify the dead.
- Henna was used to dye the hair and skin. It was also believed to ward off evil.
- The lotus symbolized Upper Egypt. As it was also a symbol of rebirth, it was used in funeral rites.

☐ Lotus

☐ Juniper

☐ Henna   ☐ Garlic   ☐ Mint   ☐ Aloe vera

Identify the amulets

Egyptians wore amulets on bracelets and necklaces. They were also placed on mummies. The three most powerful were the wedjet eye, the djed pillar, and the girdle of Isis. Can you identify which amulet is which from clues in the captions?

1. The girdle of Isis summoned the protective power of the goddess Isis. This amulet resembled a short, knotted length of cloth.

2. The djed pillar represented the god Osiris. It symbolized stability and also rebirth. This amulet was shaped like a sturdy column topped with four bars.

3. The wedjet eye provided protection against evil. It was often placed on mummies. This amulet represented the eye of the god Horus.

a.

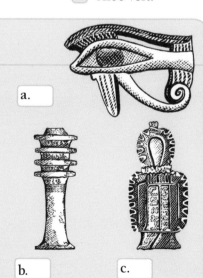

b.   c.

Scribes and Sculptors

The Egyptians excelled at both sculpture and writing. Rulers and priests commissioned sculptures honoring pharaohs and gods. Accompanying the sculptures were hieroglyphic inscriptions carved into stone. Scribes also wrote on sheets of papyrus, made from reeds. They dipped their brushes and reed pens into black ink made from soot and water.

Sculpture puzzle

Read the descriptions of three different carving styles below. Then draw a line to match each description with the correct example shown on the right.

1. Low relief are shallow carvings in flat stone. You can view them only from the front.

2. High relief are deeper carvings in flat stone, which look more three-dimensional.

3. Carvings in the round are fully three-dimensional.

a. Sculpture of a scribe

b. Carving from the temple of Hathor

c. Carving from the temple of Abu Simbel

How papyrus sheets were made

Papyrus is a triangular-stemmed reed that grew by the Nile. It was used to make paper but also ropes, sandals, baskets, and rafts.

Number the following steps in making papyrus paper in the correct order.

a. [ ] A vertical layer of strips was laid on a flat stone. Then a horizontal layer was added.

b. [ ] With the outer rind removed, the inner pith of the papyrus was sliced into strips.

c. [ ] Finally, the papyrus was polished to make a smooth surface to write on.

d. [ ] The strips were covered with a cloth and then flattened with a wooden mallet or heavy stones. Sap from the crushed pith bound the strips together.

e. [ ] Papyrus makers began by peeling off the stem's tough outer rind.

Papyrus sheet

Match the script

Draw a line to match these scripts to their descriptions. Use this page and page 13 to help.

1. Hieratic

a. This script was developed from hieroglyphs. It was faster than hieroglyphs to write and was usually written on papyrus for everyday purposes, such as letters, stories, and business contracts.

2. Demotic

b. The slowest, most elaborate form of Egyptian writing, this picture writing was carved in stone on the walls of temples and tombs and painted on religious papyri.

3. Hieroglyphs

c. This script developed last and was the fastest form of Egyptian writing. It appears with hieroglyphs and Greek on the Rosetta Stone, which was used to decipher hieroglyphs.

School for scribes

Hieroglyphs

Egyptian picture writing, or hieroglyphs, is one of the world's oldest scripts. Each hieroglyph or picture-symbol stands for an object, sound, or letter. There are more than 700 symbols in all. After 400 CE, hieroglyphs were no longer used. Their meaning was lost for 1,400 years. Then, in 1822, the French scholar Jean-François Champollion discovered how to read hieroglyphs.

Part of an inscription in hieroglyphs

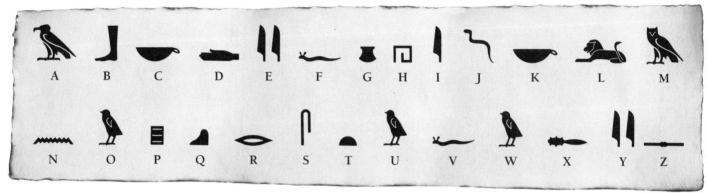

The alphabet in hieroglyphs

Write in hieroglyphs

Using the hieroglyphic alphabet above, write your name and a secret message for your friends.

Your name: ....

....

A message: ....

....

....

Did you know?

Champollion used the Rosetta Stone to decipher hieroglyphs. The Stone was discovered in 1799. It shows the same message written in three scripts: Egyptian hieroglyphs, Demotic, and Ancient Greek. Champollion could read Greek, so he looked for repeated words matched by repeated hieroglyphs.

Jean-François Champollion

Crack the code

Can you decipher this word using the hieroglyphic alphabet?

....

Temples and Priests

The Egyptians built many magnificent temples, some of which survive today. The temple of Amun-Re at Karnak, near Thebes, was the largest of all. It had more than 100 columns up to 80 ft (24 m) tall. Temples were built not as public places of worship but to house and honor the gods. Every day, processions of priests offered incense, food, and holy water to statues of the gods.

Did you know?

The temples of Abu Simbel honored three gods: Amun, Ptah, and the combined god, Re-Harakhty. This temple complex was built by Ramses II.

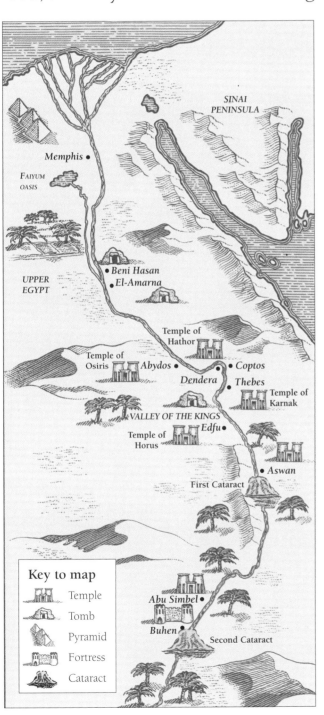

Key to map

- Temple
- Tomb
- Pyramid
- Fortress
- Cataract

Temple teaser

The map shows the location of some of Egypt's temples. Use the map and the information on this page to answer the questions below.

1. Which goddess was worshipped at Dendera, close to Thebes?
   ....
2. Which famous burial site lies north of the Temple of Horus, near Edfu?
   ....
3. Who was the chief god worshipped at Karnak, near Thebes?
   ....
4. Which temple complex lies close to the Second Cataract in Nubia, in the far south?
   ....
5. Which god had his cult center at Abydos?
   ....

A priestly procession

This illustration shows a procession led by a priest holding an incense burner and scattering purifying water. Can you number the illustration to match the descriptions?

1. Priests shaved their heads to ensure cleanliness.
2. The priest scattered water in a purifying ritual.
3. An incense burner purified the air with a pleasant fragrance to attract the god's attention.
4. Hands were raised in prayer.

c.

d.

b.

a.

Everlasting Bodies

The Egyptians preserved their dead using a process called embalming, or mummification. The stomach, lungs, liver, and intestines were removed, preserved separately, and stored in containers called canopic jars. Each jar was believed to be protected by one of the four sons of the sky god Horus. The embalmers were incredibly skilled.

Embalming puzzle

Number the three main stages of embalming in the correct order. Use the information on this page to help you.

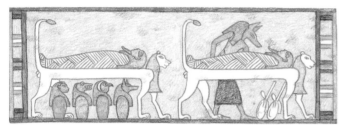

a.

The dried body was wrapped in bandages.

b.

Embalmers cleansed the body with natron salt and water.

c.

The body was packed with natron salt to dry it.

Embalming facts

- The dead body was taken to the "tent of purification" to be embalmed. It was first cleansed using natron salt dissolved in water.
- In the "place of embalming," the four most important organs and the brain were removed. The heart was left in the body.
- The body was placed on a couch and packed with natron salt to dry it.
- After 40 days, the natron salt was washed off. In the "beautiful house," the body was stuffed and anointed with perfumed oils.
- Finally, the body was covered with melted resin (tree sap) and bandaged with linen strips.

Did you know?

The Egyptians also mummified their pets, such as cats. Cats were sacred to the goddess Bastet.

What goes where?

Match the god with the canopic jar containing the organ that he guarded. The labels will help you.

1. Hapy, the baboon-headed god.
2. Qebehsenuef, the falcon-headed god.
3. Imsety, the human-headed god.
4. Duamutef, the jackal-headed god.

a.

Jar containing the stomach

b.

Jar containing the lungs

c.

Jar containing the liver

d.

Jar containing the intestines

Mummy's Case

Once embalmed, the mummy was put in its coffin. Originally just rectangular boxes, coffins became more elaborate over time. The New Kingdom pharaohs were placed inside several coffins that fitted one inside the other. Many of these cases were human-shaped. The outer coffin was placed inside a stone box called a sarcophagus.

Coffin facts

- The embalmed body was wrapped in bandages and placed in a cloth shroud.
- Protective amulets (lucky charms) were placed on the body.
- The head was covered by a mask that showed an idealized, youthful-looking portrait of the person.
- The mummy was put in an inner case, which was then placed inside an outer case. Finally, the outer case was placed in a stone sarcophagus.
- Mummy cases and tomb walls were decorated with scenes from the person's life and pictures of the gods.

Design a coffin

Design your own mummy case. You could show your hobbies, such as a sport you would hope to play in the afterlife!

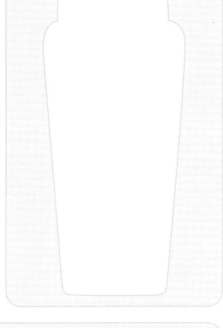

Put the mummy in its cases

Imagine you are an embalmer getting a mummy ready for burial. Number the steps in the correct order, using the information on this page to help you.

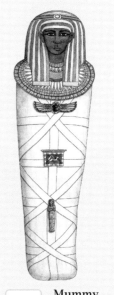

a.   Inner case

b.   Bandages and amulets

c.   Embalmed body

d.   Outer case

e.   Mummy mask

Pharaohs' Funerals

Pharaohs were buried with great pomp and ceremony. The coffin was placed on a platform called a bier and hauled to the Nile by oxen. It traveled upriver by barge. Then a long procession of priests, relatives, and hired mourners accompanied the body to the tomb, where a special ritual took place.

Funeral boat

This model of a funeral barge shows the pharaoh's mummy lying under a canopy, tended by two female mourners. Choose the right description for each label using information on this page.

Canopy   Mourner   Helmsman   Coffin   Prow

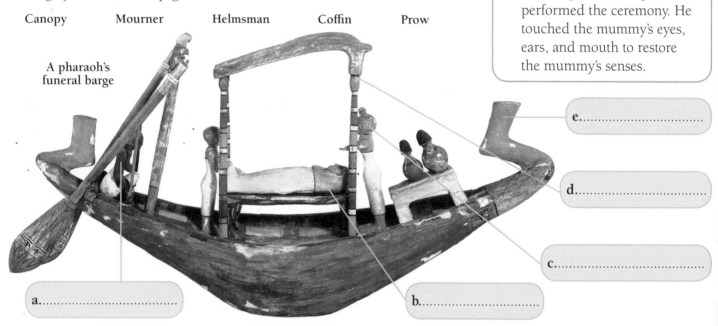

A pharaoh's funeral barge

a.......................................

b................................

c................................

d................................

e................................

Funeral facts

- Funeral barges were shaped to resemble the boat of the sun god Re. The high prow (front) and stern (rear) were carved to look like bundles of papyrus stalks.
- The helmsman at the stern steered using two long oars.
- A ritual called the Opening of the Mouth took place at the tomb entrance. It was believed to bring the mummy to life.
- The king's son, or a priest, performed the ceremony. He touched the mummy's eyes, ears, and mouth to restore the mummy's senses.

Funeral rites quiz

Circle the correct words to complete these sentences. Use the information on this page and on page 10 to help you.

1. Pharaohs were buried after **40 / 70 / 100** days of public mourning.

2. The Opening of the Mouth ceremony took place **by the tomb / in the "beautiful house" / on the Nile River.**

3. This ceremony was usually performed by the king's **mother / son / brother.**

4. Egyptians buried their dead on the outskirts of the **capital / in the desert east of the Nile / in the western desert.**

A wall painting showing the Opening of the Mouth ceremony

Journey to the Afterlife

The spirits of the dead faced a long, dangerous journey before being reborn in the afterlife. After braving fiery lakes and ferocious monsters, they arrived at the Hall of Two Truths, where they were judged by the god Osiris. The Egyptians buried their dead with all sorts of possessions they believed would come in handy in the afterlife.

Weighing of the Heart

This painting shows the heart being weighed. Draw lines to link the descriptions with the correct part of the scene. Use the information on this page to help you.

The dead man is shown dressed in white

Anubis leads the dead man into the Hall of Two Truths

Thoth writes down the result

Anubis weighs the man's heart against the feather on his scales

Ammut waits to devour the heart

Afterlife facts

- The key test for the afterlife took place in the presence of the god Osiris, lord of the underworld. The jackal-headed god Anubis weighed the dead person's heart against the feather of truth.
- If the heart weighed less than the feather, the person had lived a good life. He or she would be reborn in the next world.
- If the heart outweighed the feather, the person had done evil. The heart was devoured by the terrifying goddess Ammut, who had a crocodile's head and a hippo's back legs.
- The ibis-headed god Thoth recorded the result.

Odd one out

Grave goods included food, clothing, wigs, and jewelry. Chairs and items such as mirrors were sometimes placed in wealthy graves, along with toys, games, and musical instruments.

Draw pictures to complete this collection of burial goods and ritual instruments. Then check which of these objects is NOT put in the tomb with the dead person.

☐ **Bread**

☐ **Dates**

☐ **Cutlery**

☐ **Amulet**

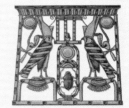

☐ **Ivory clappers**

☐ **Mirror**

☐ **Stool**

☐ **Cymbals**

The First Pyramids

The Step Pyramid at Saqqara is probably the world's oldest pyramid. It was designed as a tomb and monument for Pharaoh Djoser by the architect Imhotep. A century later, King Sneferu built three pyramids. In the course of their construction, pyramids evolved from the step design to having even, sloping sides.

Label the Step Pyramid

Number the labels to match the descriptions of the Step Pyramid below.
Use the information on this page to help you.

1. The pyramid rises in six tiers to 198 ft (60 m) high.
2. The bottom step of the pyramid is more than 330 ft (100 m) long.
3. There is only one real gateway in the walls. Fake entrances fooled intruders.
4. The South Courtyard is the largest enclosed space, used for ceremonies.
5. Small chapels with rounded roofs are also fakes, filled with rubble.

Early pyramid facts

- The Step Pyramid complex includes several courtyards and many chapels. The outer wall has 15 doors but only one is real.
- Sneferu's first pyramid, at Meidum, was designed as a step pyramid and then given straight sides.
- Sneferu's second pyramid, the Bent Pyramid, has sides that slope steeply at the base but are flatter near the top.
- Sneferu's third pyramid is called the Red Pyramid, because of its color.

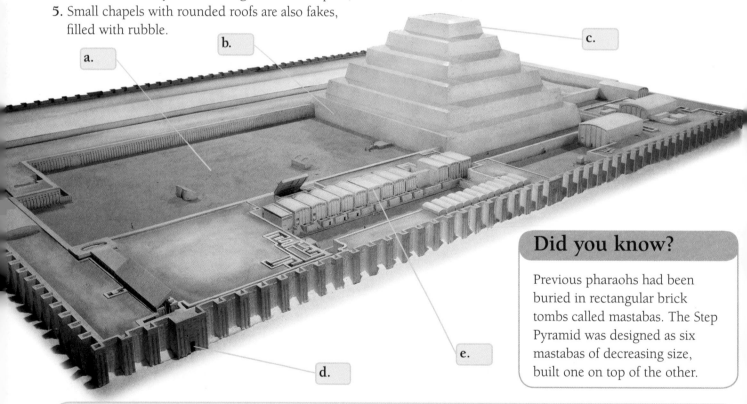

a.
b.
c.
d.
e.

Did you know?

Previous pharaohs had been buried in rectangular brick tombs called mastabas. The Step Pyramid was designed as six mastabas of decreasing size, built one on top of the other.

Early pyramid puzzle

Number these pyramids in date order, starting with the earliest.
Use the information on this page and on page 11 to help you.

a. Bent Pyramid   b. Red Pyramid   c. Step Pyramid   d. Meidum Pyramid

Later Pyramids

The Great Pyramid was commissioned by Sneferu's son, Khufu. Built in about 2580 BCE during Old Kingdom times, it was the world's tallest building for more than 4,000 years. Pyramids were also built during the Middle Kingdom, but to a cheaper design, with an outer stone casing covering an inner core of mud bricks.

The Sphinx guards the Great Pyramid

Explore the Great Pyramid

Choose from the descriptions below to label this diagram of the Great Pyramid.

Limestone casing

King's Chamber

Queen's Chamber

Grand Gallery

Original chamber

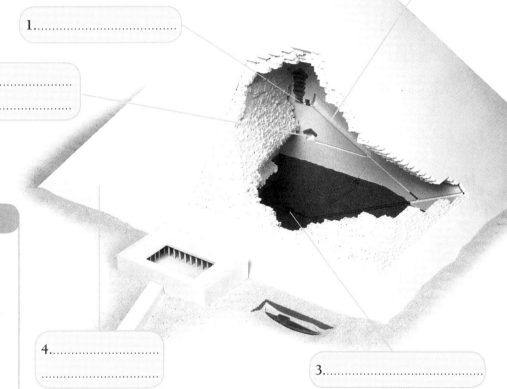

1. ....

2. ....
....

5. ....
....

4. ....
....

3. ....

Great Pyramid facts

• The inner structure of the Great Pyramid changed three times. The original burial chamber was built at the base. A second chamber, also unused, lies near the center. It is sometimes called the Queen's Chamber. Above this is the King's Chamber, where Khufu's body was finally laid.

• The King's Chamber is topped with five cavities designed to support the great weight of the stones above.

• The high-roofed passage leading to the King's Chamber is called the Grand Gallery.

• The Great Pyramid was originally faced with fine white limestone, but much later this was removed to build the nearby city of Cairo.

Pyramid maze

Middle Kingdom pyramids were designed with many false doors and passages that led nowhere. The aim was to foil tomb robbers. Can you find your way through the maze inside this pyramid plan to reach the pharaoh's tomb?

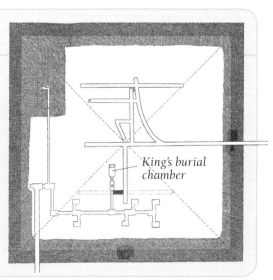

King's burial chamber

— *Blocked passage*

Plan of a pyramid

Pyramid Building

The pyramids are amazing achievements that involved enormous effort, time, and expense. They also needed very careful planning, with detailed drawings and calculations by skilled architects. The Great Pyramid at Giza is made up of about 2.3 million limestone blocks, each weighing as much as a family car. The huge stones were hauled into place without pulleys, cranes, or other machinery.

Stages in building a pyramid

Number the pictures in the correct order, using information on this page.

a. **Transporting blocks for the outer casing by barge**

d. **Transporting construction blocks by sledge**

b. **Dismantling the ramp**

e. **Smoothing the casing blocks' outer face**

c. **Dragging blocks up the ramps**

f. **Quarrying blocks of stone for construction**

Did you know?

The pyramids at Giza are the oldest of the Seven Wonders of the Ancient World, and the only ones left. They were already more than 1,000 years old and a tourist attraction in Tutankhamun's day.

Building facts

- The coarse limestone used to construct the core of the pyramid came from a nearby quarry at Giza.
- Workers quarried the stone blocks by hammering wooden wedges into solid rock. Water poured over the wedges made them swell and split the rock.
- Blocks were then hauled to the rising pyramid by sledge.
- Fine limestone for the outer casing was ferried from a quarry across the Nile by barge. Granite for the burial chamber came by barge from Aswan, far to the south.
- Workers dragged the blocks up the pyramid using ramps—maybe one ramp, which gradually grew higher and longer, or a series of ramps spiraling around the pyramid.
- A capstone topped the pyramid in a perfect point.
- Then the workers started to dismantle the ramp from the top down, by hurling baskets of rubble over the side.
- As they worked their way down, stonemasons smoothed the outer facing with copper chisels. The pyramid shone!

Valley of the Kings

New Kingdom pharaohs ruled from the city of Thebes. Their kings were buried in a secret valley across the Nile, now called the Valley of the Kings. By the 1920s, archaeologists had excavated more than 60 tombs there, but all their treasure had been robbed. Then in 1922, British archaeologist Howard Carter discovered the hidden tomb of Tutankhamun, containing fabulous treasure.

Valley of the Kings

Valley of the Kings puzzle

Study the map and decide whether the following statements are true or false.

	TRUE	FALSE
1. Queen Hatshepsut is buried close to her relative, Tuthmosis IV.	☐	☐
2. Cleopatra VII was buried in the Valley of the Kings.	☐	☐
3. The tomb of Tuthmosis III lies in the southwest corner of the valley.	☐	☐
4. The tomb of Tutankhamun lies beneath the tomb of Ramesses II.	☐	☐

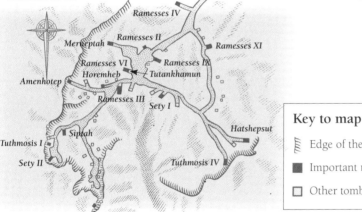

Key to map
- 〰 Edge of the valley
- ■ Important royal tombs
- ☐ Other tombs and burial pits

Explore Tutankhamun's tomb

Look at the diagram of Tutankhamun's tomb and the list of the four main rooms. First match each room to the correct letter on the diagram.

- ...../..... **Burial chamber**
- ...../..... **Annex**
- ...../..... **Treasury**
- ...../..... **Antechamber**

Now number the rooms in the order they were excavated, starting with the first.

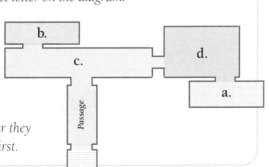

Tutankhamun's tomb

- The Valley of the Kings is hidden by steep cliffs. The narrow entrance could be guarded against tomb robbers.
- In 1922, Howard Carter discovered Tutankhamun's tomb beneath the tomb of Ramses VI. Steps led down to a passage with a sealed door.
- Carter broke through the door to find an antechamber containing gilded furniture. He excavated this room first.
- A door on the right-hand wall of the antechamber led to the burial chamber, containing four gilded shrines, one inside another. These held the coffins, mummy, and famous mask of the king.
- Having excavated the burial chamber, Carter moved on to the room beyond, called the treasury because it was piled with priceless objects.
- The last room to be excavated was a small annex that led off the antechamber. This held yet more treasure, including furniture and model boats.
- The short-lived pharaoh now became the most famous of all.

War and Weapons

In the early days, Egypt had a small army. The desert and sea to the north protected the country from attack. In later years, Egypt's wealth attracted raiders. After an attack by the Hyksos in 1630 BCE, the Egyptian army became larger and better equipped. Warrior kings such as Tuthmosis III and Ramses II led their troops to victory in battle.

Warriors' weapons

This drawing shows Egyptian soldiers armed with a variety of weapons.
Label the weapons using the information on this page. Choose from this list.

Spear   Kopesh   Cudgel   Bow   Metpenet

1.....................

2.....................

3.....................

4.....................

5.....................

Military facts

- In the Old Kingdom, Egyptian soldiers carried a short spear. Some men had bows, shields, and short stabbing swords called metpenets.

- Light, easily managed chariots were introduced after the Hyksos attack. They carried a charioteer and an archer.

- Later weapons included a stronger bow and a curved sword called a kopesh. Soldiers had stronger shields, and leather and metal armor.

- In New Kingdom times, the pharaoh was commander in chief. His fighting units were named after gods such as Re and Amun.

- Egypt also had a fleet of ships. These carried a square sail but were mainly powered by oar.

- Egyptians used the same word for army and task force. In peacetime, soldiers performed civil duties—quarrying stone, digging irrigation trenches, and building the pyramids.

Army quiz

Circle the correct words to complete these statements about the Egyptian army. Use the information on this page to help you.

1. Army divisions were named after **the pharaoh** / **a god** / **the division commander.**

2. A kopesh was a bronze-tipped **spear** / **heavy cudgel** / **curved sword.**

3. Chariots carried two men: a charioteer and a **swordsman** / **archer** / **spearman.**

4. Egyptian warships were mainly powered by **oars** / **a single square sail** / **a triangular sail.**

Tutankhamun's war chariot

Painting and Portraits

Egyptian artists and craftsmen made beautiful wall paintings, sculptures, and furniture. They also made jewelry from gold and semiprecious stones. The finest art was produced for the royal tombs, which had pictures of gods and everyday scenes. Tomb art was not just decoration—people believed the scenes would come to life in the next world.

Children were pictured smaller but had the same body proportions as adults

Family portrait of a couple and their two children

Paint an Egyptian-style portrait

Make an Egyptian-style portrait of a friend sitting on a chair. Look at the pictures and information on this page and follow the steps below.

1 Mark the proportions for the seated figure in pencil. First draw lines 0.5 in (1 cm) apart, down and across your paper, to make a grid of squares.

2 From the top of the head to the shoulders is 3 squares. Make an oval for the head.

3 Mark the distance between the chin and the seat of the chair, which equals 7 squares.

4 Mark the distance between the seat and the floor, which equals 5 squares, making the whole figure 15 squares tall from head to toe.

5 Now sketch your friend in pencil. Show their figure in profile but with eyes and shoulders facing forward.

6 Ink in the outline and rub out all pencil marks. Now color your drawing using colored pencils, crayons, or paints.

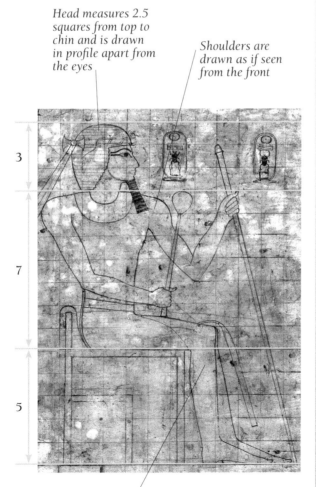

Head measures 2.5 squares from top to chin and is drawn in profile apart from the eyes

Shoulders are drawn as if seen from the front

Lower part of the body is drawn in profile

Wooden drawing board marked with a grid, showing Tuthmosis III

Arty facts

- Artists followed strict rules for portraits. Most of the body was shown in profile (side on), but eyes, shoulders, and chest were drawn front on.

- Sculptors and artists carved and painted portraits of the dead looking youthful so that they would look young in the afterlife.

- Before painting a tomb wall, artists first marked out a grid of squares to make sure all parts of the body would be shown in proportion.

* A master craftsman drew outlines of the figures, which were checked by a supervisor.

* Then assistants colored the images with paint. Egyptian paints were made from natural materials such as minerals. Black pigment (paint) was made from charcoal, white from chalk, red from iron oxide, and blue from copper or lapis lazuli.

Fashion and Makeup

Egyptian clothes were stylish yet practical. Fine white linen clothes made from flax fiber were cool in hot weather. Women wore long, simple shift dresses. Men wore calf-length skirts or shifts. People put on warm cloaks for chilly evenings.

Make a bracelet

Egyptian jewelers made necklaces and girdles by stringing semiprecious stones and golden charms onto papyrus twine.

Part of an Egyptian girdle strung with lucky charms

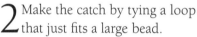

Gold fish amulet prevents drowning

Beard or sidelock represents youth

Lapis lazuli bead

Coral bead

A god of long life

Gold cowrie shell brings fertility

1 You can make a similar necklace by stringing beads, shells, and lucky charms onto twine or fishing line.

2 Make the catch by tying a loop that just fits a large bead.

Did you know?

Men and women wore jewelry such as necklaces, wide collars, bracelets, and rings. This ring has a swiveling stone carved with a scarab beetle for good luck.

Fashion facts

- Egyptian makeup was made from crushed minerals or plants mixed with oil or water. Eyeliner was made of charcoal. Women colored their lips and cheeks with red ocher.

- Many men and women shaved their heads and wore wigs in public. At banquets, women wore cones of perfumed oil on top of their wigs. The oil melted in the heat and ran down their clothes.

- Hygiene was important. Ordinary people washed in the Nile, while nobles bathed in water perfumed with oil.

- Mirrors were made from polished copper or bronze.

Fashion quiz

Cone of perfumed oil

Answer these questions using information on this page and on page 12.

1. What plant did the Egyptians use to make linen?
   ....

2. What did the Egyptians use to make dark eyeliner for their eyes?
   ....

3. How did children wear their hair?
   ....

4. What did Egyptian ladies wear to make themselves smell nice at banquets?
   ....

5. What were Egyptians mirrors made from?
   ....

Lady applying eyeliner

Food and Feasts

Most Egyptians ate two meals a day—a breakfast of bread and beer, and a main meal in the afternoon. Some wealthy people ate three meals: breakfast, lunch, and a main evening meal. Banquets were lavish affairs for the rich, with courses such as whole roast oxen, duck, geese, and fish. There was also fruit such as grapes and figs, sweet cakes, and flagons of wine.

Banquet scene

Match the correct labels to this illustration of a banquet thrown by Antony and Cleopatra.

a.
b.
c.
d.
e.
f.

1. A servant brings a roasted boar head. Unless cooked and eaten immediately, meats were preserved by salting or drying to last in the hot climate.
2. A servant keeps guests cool with an ostrich-plume fan.
3. Guests lounged on couches and ate with the right hand.
4. Musicians play stringed and wind instruments and keep time using rattles, clappers, tambourines, and castanets.
5. Acrobats provided entertainment at banquets and religious festivals.
6. Wine is served from flagons, but ordinary people mostly drank beer.

What is it made from?

Draw lines to match these foods to the products they are made from. Use the information on page 12 to help you.

1. Wine   a. Wheat
2. Bread   b. Barley
3. Beer   c. Grapes

Grapes   Bread

Egyptian date cakes

Egyptians liked sweet foods. This is one of the world's oldest recipes and was found written on a clay tablet. It is made with dates and nuts.

Dates

You will need:
- 7 oz (200 g) fresh dates, stones removed
- cinnamon
- chopped walnuts
- honey
- ground almonds

1 Chop and mash the dates with a little water.

2 Add a little cinnamon and chopped walnuts to taste.

3 Shape the mixture into balls, with your fingers or a spoon.

4 Coat the balls in honey mixed with ground almonds, and serve. Delicious!

Markets and Trade

Egypt's barter system was based on trading items of equal value. Every product had a known value. For example, a goat was worth 4 deben weight of copper. At markets, people traded foods such as meat, bread, beer, and barley for manufactured goods such as sandals, robes, furniture, and tools.

Market day puzzle

Imagine you are a farmer going to market with your harvest of barley. Barley and other grain is traded in units of volume called hekats. Your harvest of 50 hekats is worth 13 kite of silver. You buy a bronze cauldron worth 3 kite of silver. With your remaining barley, you want to buy cloth, which can be traded for 1 deben of copper per cubit, to make robes for your family. Five kite of silver is worth 8 deben of copper. How many cubits of cloth can you trade your barley for?

....

Some Egyptian weights were shaped like animals

Gold

Animal-shaped weights

Scales were used to weigh goods at the market

Trade facts

- Cloth was traded in a unit of length called a cubit.
- A deben weighed around 3 oz (91 g). A smaller weight called a kite was used for valuable goods, such as silver and gold.
- Egypt produced wheat, barley, flax, copper, papyrus, and wine. These were traded within Egypt and with foreign lands.
- Animals reared for meat included cattle, sheep, goats, ducks, and geese. Bees were kept for honey.
- Silver, cedarwood, and horses came from the Middle East.
- Cassia bark, used to make perfume, came from India.
- A blue stone called lapis lazuli from Afghanistan was used to make jewelry.
- Nubia to the south produced gold, ivory, ebony, and spices.
- Fragrant frankincense and myrrh came from the mysterious African land of Punt, far to the south.

Which goods were imported?

Check the products NOT made in Egypt but brought from foreign lands. Use the information on this page to help you.

☐ Cow

☐ Copper

☐ Cassia bark

☐ Barley

☐ Lapis lazuli

☐ Cedarwood

☐ Papyrus

☐ Ivory tusk

Living on the Nile

The Nile was Egypt's highway. Boats were used for transporting everything from crops and building stones to the pharaoh's coffin. People also sailed for pleasure and hunted animals along the banks. Egyptian boats were originally made of reeds. Later, cedarwood was used to make more substantial craft. Early boats were powered by oars. Later, sails were invented.

Hunting facts

- Abundant wildlife of the Nile included fish, waterfowl, crocodiles, and hippos. Beasts such as jackals, lion, and antelope came to drink.
- Noblemen went hunting for sport. They stunned waterbirds using curved throwing sticks.
- Professional fishermen caught fish using hooks and also nets weighted with stones.
- Dangerous beasts such as hippos were hunted using spears and lassos. Fast-moving hares and antelope were brought down with arrows.

Hunting equipment

Using the information on this page, draw lines to match the type of equipment or weapon that was used to hunt each animal.

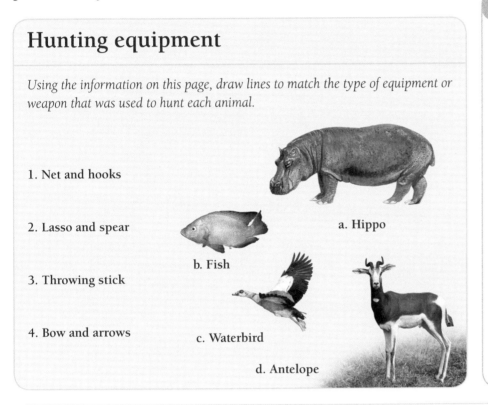

1. Net and hooks

2. Lasso and spear

3. Throwing stick

4. Bow and arrows

a. Hippo

b. Fish

c. Waterbird

d. Antelope

Sailing on the Nile

This model boat came from an Egyptian tomb. Number the labels to match the descriptions below, using information on this page and on page 26.

1. To travel south, which was against the river's flow, sailors pulled on rigging to raise a sail.
2. If the boat grounded on the uneven, muddy riverbed, sailors pushed the boat off with poles.
3. A helmsman at the stern steered the boat with a large oar.
4. The owner of the boat was shaded from the fierce desert sun by an ox-hide canopy.
5. Sailors used a weighted line called a plumb line to check the water depth.

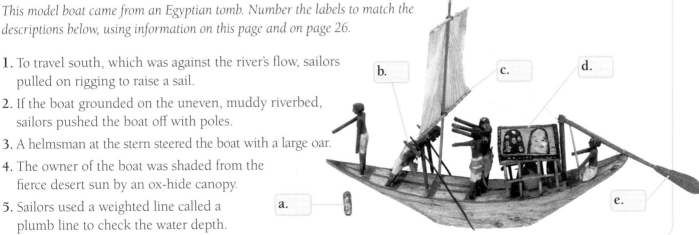

The Pharaohs

Check or number the boxes to answer each question. Check your answers on page 46.

1 The kingdoms of Upper and Lower Egypt were united:

- ☐ **a.** Around 4000 BCE
- ☐ **b.** Around 3100 BCE
- ☐ **c.** Around 2100 BCE
- ☐ **d.** Around 1200 BCE

2 Egypt's legendary ruler who united the two kingdoms was named:

- ☐ **a.** Djoser
- ☐ **b.** Khufu
- ☐ **c.** Akhenaten
- ☐ **d.** Narmer

3 The word pharaoh means:

- ☐ **a.** Prince of Thebes
- ☐ **b.** Great house
- ☐ **c.** Son of Re
- ☐ **d.** Foremost prince

4 Which pharaoh is the odd one out, who did not rule in New Kingdom times:

- ☐ **a.** Khufu
- ☐ **b.** Tutankhamun
- ☐ **c.** Ramses II
- ☐ **d.** Akhenaten

5 List these kings in order by date, starting with the earliest:

- ☐ **a.** Ramses II
- ☐ **b.** Ptolemy XII
- ☐ **c.** Narmer
- ☐ **d.** Tutankhamun
- ☐ **e.** Djoser

6 The striped headdress worn by pharaoh was called the:

- ☐ **a.** Nome
- ☐ **b.** Blue crown
- ☐ **c.** Nemes cloth
- ☐ **d.** Diadem of Re

7 The pharaoh who ruled for longest was:

- ☐ **a.** Tuthmosis III
- ☐ **b.** Ramses II
- ☐ **c.** Hatshepsut
- ☐ **d.** Pepy II

8 The only pharaoh whose tomb was found intact was:

- ☐ **a.** Khufu
- ☐ **b.** Tutankhamun
- ☐ **c.** Hatshepsut
- ☐ **d.** Cleopatra

9 Akhenaten's queen was named:

- ☐ **a.** Ankhesenamun
- ☐ **b.** Neferure
- ☐ **c.** Hatshepsut
- ☐ **d.** Nefertiti

10 Cleopatra's father was:

- ☐ **a.** Ptolemy XII
- ☐ **b.** Ptolemy XIII
- ☐ **c.** Julius Caesar
- ☐ **d.** Caesarion

Religion

Check or number the boxes to answer each question. Check your answers on page 46.

1 The god Anubis was shown with the head of a:

☐ a. Lion
☐ b. Crocodile
☐ c. Jackal
☐ d. Cow

2 The god Osiris was married to his sister:

☐ a. Hathor
☐ b. Isis
☐ c. Sekhmet
☐ d. Bastet

3 Which god is the odd one out, not worshipped in ancient Egypt?

☐ a. Horus
☐ b. Re
☐ c. Zeus
☐ d. Osiris

4 The patron of doctors and healing was:

☐ a. Thoth
☐ b. Ptah
☐ c. Re
☐ d. Khepri

5 Which animal is the odd one out, not a symbol of an Egyptian god or goddess?

☐ a. Scarab beetle
☐ b. Ibis
☐ c. Jackal
☐ d. Tiger

6 The goddess Bastet was associated with:

☐ a. Hippos
☐ b. Crocodiles
☐ c. Lions
☐ d. Cats

7 The girdle of which goddess featured in a lucky charm, believed to ward off evil?

☐ a. Isis
☐ b. Hathor
☐ c. Sekhmet
☐ d. Ammut

8 Select anyone allowed to enter Egyptian temples:

☐ a. priestesses
☐ b. pharaohs
☐ c. wealthy landowners
☐ d. priests
☐ e. farmers

9 The pharaoh who built the temples at Abu Simbel was:

☐ a. Hatshepsut
☐ b. Khufu
☐ c. Ramses II
☐ d. Sneferu

10 Egypt's largest temple was built at:

☐ a. Dendera
☐ b. Karnak
☐ c. Abu Simbel
☐ d. Edfu

11 Which god or godddess had a cult center at Dendera:

☐ a. Hathor
☐ b. Khnum
☐ c. Horus
☐ d. Anubis

Mummification and the Afterlife

Check or number the boxes to answer each question. Check your answers on page 46.

1 List the steps of mummification in the right order:

☐ **a.** The dried body was taken to the beautiful house.
☐ **b.** The corpse was cleansed in the tent of purification.
☐ **c.** The body was packed in natron salt to dry it.
☐ **d.** The mummy was wrapped in strips of linen.
☐ **e.** The dried body was anointed with perfumed oils.

2 Select any of the organs that were removed and preserved separately:

☐ **a.** Liver
☐ **b.** Eyes
☐ **c.** Stomach
☐ **d.** Heart
☐ **e.** Intestines

3 The Egyptians preserved certain organs in containers called:

☐ **a.** Canopic jars
☐ **b.** Vessels of Osiris
☐ **c.** Pots of Anubis
☐ **d.** Jars of Ammut

4 Egyptian embalmers dried the corpse for:

☐ **a.** 10 days
☐ **b.** 40 days
☐ **c.** 70 days
☐ **d.** 100 days

5 The place where the corpse was anointed was called:

☐ **a.** The place of embalming
☐ **b.** The land of the dead
☐ **c.** The tent of purification
☐ **d.** The beautiful house

6 The god of embalming was:

☐ **a.** Thoth
☐ **b.** Re
☐ **c.** Anubis
☐ **d.** Bes

7 The outer stone coffin was called a:

☐ **a.** Sarcophagus
☐ **b.** Shrine
☐ **c.** Scarab case
☐ **d.** Tomb

8 The ceremony believed to restore a dead person's senses was called the:

☐ **a.** Opening of the mouth
☐ **b.** Weighing of the heart
☐ **c.** Removing of the organs
☐ **d.** Anointing of the body

9 To pass to the next life, the spirit had to undergo a trial called the:

☐ **a.** Testing of the brain
☐ **b.** Opening of the mouth
☐ **c.** Seeking of the truth
☐ **d.** Weighing of the heart

10 The underworld ruled by Osiris was called:

☐ **a.** Duat
☐ **b.** Karnak
☐ **c.** Giza
☐ **d.** The Valley of the Kings

Pyramids

Check or number the boxes to answer each question. Check your answers on page 46.

1 Egypt's first pyramid was the:

- [ ] **a.** Great Pyramid
- [ ] **b.** Step Pyramid
- [ ] **c.** Bent Pyramid
- [ ] **d.** Khafre's Pyramid
- [ ] **e.** Louvre Pyramid

2 Egypt's first pyramid was designed by:

- [ ] **a.** Djoser
- [ ] **b.** Khufu
- [ ] **c.** Imhotep
- [ ] **d.** Sneferu

3 Which pharaoh built three pyramids, all to different designs?

- [ ] **a.** Sneferu
- [ ] **b.** Tutankhamun
- [ ] **c.** Pepy II
- [ ] **d.** Tuthmosis III

4 List these pyramid-building pharaohs in order by date, starting with the earliest:

- [ ] **a.** Khafre
- [ ] **b.** Sneferu
- [ ] **c.** Khufu
- [ ] **d.** Djoser

5 The golden age of pyramid building was the:

- [ ] **a.** Old Kingdom
- [ ] **b.** Middle Kingdom
- [ ] **c.** New Kingdom
- [ ] **d.** Ptolemaic Era

6 Egypt's largest pyramid is found at:

- [ ] **a.** Saqqara
- [ ] **b.** Giza
- [ ] **c.** Alexandria
- [ ] **d.** Karnak

7 Which pharaoh is the odd one out, who did not build a pyramid at Giza?

- [ ] **a.** Khufu
- [ ] **b.** Sneferu
- [ ] **c.** Menkaura
- [ ] **d.** Khafre

8 Select all the items used to build the pyramids:

- [ ] **a.** Pulleys
- [ ] **b.** Wooden sledges
- [ ] **c.** Ramps
- [ ] **d.** Ropes
- [ ] **e.** Cranes

9 The head of the Sphinx at Giza is thought to be a portrait of:

- [ ] **a.** Menkaura
- [ ] **b.** Imhotep
- [ ] **c.** Khafre
- [ ] **d.** Djoser

10 A sphinx has the body of a:

- [ ] **a.** Hippo
- [ ] **b.** Antelope
- [ ] **c.** Ibis
- [ ] **d.** Lion

11 Which pyramid contains three burial chambers, two of which were never used?

- [ ] **a.** Bent Pyramid
- [ ] **b.** Great Pyramid
- [ ] **c.** Red Pyramid
- [ ] **d.** Step Pyramid

Writing, Arts, and Crafts

Check or number the boxes to answer each question. Check your answers on page 46.

1 Egyptian hieroglyphs were invented around:

- ☐ **a.** 2300 BCE
- ☐ **b.** 3300 BCE
- ☐ **c.** 1200 BCE
- ☐ **d.** 100 CE

2 The god who was believed to have given the gift of writing to the Egyptians was:

- ☐ **a.** Khepri
- ☐ **b.** Thoth
- ☐ **c.** Horus
- ☐ **d.** Anubis

3 Professional writers were called:

- ☐ **a.** regents
- ☐ **b.** viziers
- ☐ **c.** scribes
- ☐ **d.** nomarchs

4 The total number of symbols used in hieroglyphics was over:

- ☐ **a.** 100
- ☐ **b.** 200
- ☐ **c.** 500
- ☐ **d.** 700

5 Select all the directions in which hieroglyphs could read:

- ☐ **a.** left to right
- ☐ **b.** right to left
- ☐ **c.** top to bottom
- ☐ **d.** bottom to top

6 The secret of hieroglyphics was finally cracked in:

- ☐ **a.** 2002
- ☐ **b.** 1722
- ☐ **c.** 1922
- ☐ **d.** 1822

7 Hieroglyphics were decoded with a help of an inscription on the:

- ☐ **a.** Hyksos Stone
- ☐ **b.** Stone of Destiny
- ☐ **c.** Rosetta Stone
- ☐ **d.** Stone of Scone

8 Order the stages of tomb painting:

- ☐ **a.** The outlines were checked by a supervisor
- ☐ **b.** The supervisor marked any corrections that were needed.
- ☐ **c.** A principal artist drew outlines of hieroglyphs and figures.
- ☐ **d.** Assistants colored in the outlines.
- ☐ **e.** A draftsman marked out a grid of squares.
- ☐ **f.** The wall was smoothed to provide an even surface to paint on.

9 Check all the parts of the body shown from the front in tomb paintings:

- ☐ **a.** Eyes
- ☐ **b.** Hips
- ☐ **c.** Shoulders
- ☐ **d.** Mouth
- ☐ **e.** Feet

10 Egyptian papyrus sheets were made from:

- ☐ **a.** cedarwood
- ☐ **b.** river reeds
- ☐ **c.** juniper
- ☐ **d.** lotus stems

11 Craftspeople often carved rings and amulets in the shape of an insect. Which one?

- ☐ **a.** praying mantis
- ☐ **b.** purple emperor butterfly
- ☐ **c.** bee
- ☐ **d.** scarab beetle
- ☐ **e.** ladybug

Daily Life

Check or number the boxes to answer each question. Check your answers on page 46.

1 Select the activities enjoyed by children in ancient Egypt:

- ☐ **a.** sailing
- ☐ **b.** fishing
- ☐ **c.** skateboarding
- ☐ **d.** storytelling
- ☐ **e.** gymnastics
- ☐ **f.** board games

2 How old did Egyptian men tend to be when they got married?

- ☐ **a.** 14–15
- ☐ **b.** 16–18
- ☐ **c.** 19–21
- ☐ **d.** 22–30

3 Tick the odd one out, a type of fruit not eaten in ancient Egypt:

- ☐ **a.** dates
- ☐ **b.** figs
- ☐ **c.** bananas
- ☐ **d.** grapes

4 What fabric did the ancient Egyptians use for clothing worn in hot weather?

- ☐ **a.** wool
- ☐ **b.** cotton
- ☐ **c.** linen
- ☐ **d.** nylon

5 The fertile strip of land watered by the Nile was called the:

- ☐ **a.** Red Land
- ☐ **b.** Black Land
- ☐ **c.** Green Land
- ☐ **d.** Yellow Land

6 Select all the items made from papyrus:

- ☐ **a.** boats
- ☐ **b.** bricks
- ☐ **c.** sandals
- ☐ **d.** linen
- ☐ **e.** ropes

7 Select all the animals hunted along the Nile:

- ☐ **a.** tiger
- ☐ **b.** hippo
- ☐ **c.** antelope
- ☐ **d.** waterfowl
- ☐ **e.** polar bear

8 Check all the boxes showing uses of boats in ancient Egypt:

- ☐ **a.** carrying wheat
- ☐ **b.** transporting the king's coffin
- ☐ **c.** irrigation
- ☐ **d.** sailing for pleasure
- ☐ **e.** transporting stone

9 Check the product not produced in Egypt but brought from abroad:

- ☐ **a.** frankincense
- ☐ **b.** copper
- ☐ **c.** wine
- ☐ **d.** papyrus

10 A deben was a:

- ☐ **a.** carpentry tool
- ☐ **b.** measurement of land
- ☐ **c.** short sword
- ☐ **d.** unit of weight

11 The purple stone from Afghanistan used in jewelry was called:

- ☐ **a.** topaz
- ☐ **b.** lapis lazuli
- ☐ **c.** garnet
- ☐ **d.** carnelian

Activity Answers

Once you have completed each page of activities, check your answers below.

Page 14
Complete the farming calendar
1 Inundation
2 Growing season
3 Harvest

Color the map

Page 15
Complete the social pyramid

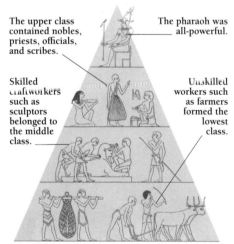

The upper class contained nobles, priests, officials, and scribes.

The pharaoh was all-powerful.

Skilled craftworkers such as sculptors belonged to the middle class.

Unskilled workers such as farmers formed the lowest class.

Page 15
Symbols of rule
a 3
b 4
c 1
d 2

Page 16
Tutankhamun family quiz
1 True
2 False
3 False
4 True

Order Tutankhamun's life story
1 c   4 d
2 e   5 b
3 a

Page 17
Who is who?
1 Ramses II
2 Tuthmosis III
3 Hatshepsut
4 Khufu

Hatshepsut's family tree
a Wadjmose
b Amenose
c Akhbetneferu
d Tuthmosis II
e Tuthmosis III
f Neferure

Page 18
Life of Cleopatra
a 4   e 1
b 5   f 6
c 2   g 3
d 7

Cleopatra Quiz
1 Mark Antony
2 four
3 using a poisonous snake

Order the queens
a 4   c 3
b 2   d 1

Page 19
Whose symbol?
Scarab beetle	Khepri
Ibis	Thoth
Ram	Khnum
Cow	Hathor
Cat	Bastet
Jackal	Anubis

Who would you pray to?
1 Sekhmet
2 Ptah
3 Thoth
4 Hathor
5 Bastet

Page 20
Select the magic plants
lotus, juniper, garlic, henna

Identify the amulets
1 c
2 b
3 a

Page 21
Sculpture puzzle
1 b
2 c
3 a

How papyrus sheets were made
a 3   d 4
b 2   e 1
c 5

Match the script
1 a
2 c
3 b

Page 22
Write in hieroglyphs
Hint: You could arrange the letters to read left to right, right to left, or in a vertical column, to read from top to bottom.

Crack the code
R O S E T T A

Page 23
Temple teaser
1 Hathor
2 Valley of the Kings
3 Amun-Re
4 Abu Simbel
5 Osiris

A priestly procession
a 2   c 4
b 3   d 1

Page 24
Embalming puzzle
a 3   b 1   c 2

What goes where?
a 4   c 3
b 1   d 2

Page 25
Put the mummy in its cases
a 4   d 5
b 2   e 3
c 1

Page 26
Funeral boat
a Helmsman   d Canopy
b Coffin   e Prow
c Mourner

Funeral rites quiz
1 70
2 by the tomb
3 son
4 in the western desert

Page 27
Weighing of the heart

The dead man is shown dressed in white.

Anubis leads the dead man into the Hall of Two Truths.

Thoth writes down the result.

Anubis weighs the man's heart against the feather on his scales.

Ammut waits to devour the heart.

Odd one out
Cutlery is the odd one out. Ancient Egyptians took everything they needed for the afterlife, but they didn't need cutlery—they ate with their fingers.

Page 28
Label the Step Pyramid
1 b   4 a
2 d   5 e
3 c

Early pyramid puzzle
a 3   c 1
b 4   d 2

Page 29
Explore the Great Pyramid
1 King's Chamber
2 Grand Gallery
3 Original chamber
4 Limestone casing
5 Queen's Chamber

Pyramid maze

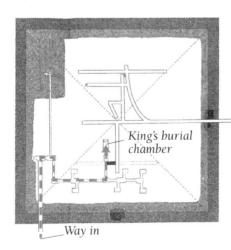

King's burial chamber

Way in

Page 30
Stages in building a pyramid
a 3
b 5
c 4
d 2
e 6
f 1

Page 31
Valley of the Kings Puzzle
1 True
2 False—Cleopatra's final resting place has never been found.
3 True
4 False—Tutankhamun's tomb is beneath the tomb of Ramses VI.

Explore Tutankhamun's tomb
Burial chamber   d / 2
Annex   b / 4
Treasury   a / 3
Antechamber   c / 1

Page 32
Warriors' weapons
1 spear
2 bow
3 cudgel
4 metpenet
5 kopesh

Army quiz
1 a god
2 curved sword
3 archer
4 oars

Page 34
Fashion quiz
1 Flax
2 Charcoal
3 Shaved except for one or more long locks
4 Perfumed cones on their heads
5 Polished copper or bronze

Page 35
Banquet scene
a 2   d 4
b 6   e 3
c 5   f 1

What is it made from?
1 c   2 a   3 b

Page 36
Market day puzzle
The answer is 16 cubits of cloth. You need to trade 3 kite worth of barley in exchange for the cauldron, leaving you 10 kite worth of barley. This 10 kite worth is equivalent to 16 deben of copper, which would buy you cloth measuring 16 cubits, which is enough to make robes for a small family.

Page 36
Which goods were imported?
ivory
cedarwood
lapis lazuli
cassia bark

Page 37
Hunting equipment
1 b	3 c
2 a	4 d

Sailing on the Nile
1 c	4 d
2 b	5 a
3 e	

Quick Quiz Answers
Once you have completed each page of quiz questions, check your answers below.

page 38
The Pharaohs
1 b 2 d 3 b 4 a 5 a4, b5, c1, d3, e2
6 c 7 d 8 b 9 d 10 a

page 39
Religion
1 c 2 b 3 c 4 b 5 d 6 d 7 a
8 a, b, d 9 c 10 b 11 a

page 40
Mummification and the Afterlife
1 a3, b1, c2, d5, e4 2 a, c, e 3 a 4 b
5 d 6 c 7 a 8 a 9 d 10 a

page 41
Pyramids
1 b 2 c 3 a 4 a4, b2, c3, d1 5 a
6 b 7 b 8 b, c, d 9 c 10 d 11 b

page 42
Writing, Arts, and Crafts
1 b 2 b 3 c 4 d 5 a, b, c 6 d 7 c
8 a4, b5, c3, d6, e2, f1 9 a, c 10 b
11 d

page 43
Daily Life
1 a, b, d, e, f 2 a 3 c 4 c 5 b
6 a, c, e 7 b, c, d 8 a, b, d, e 9 a
10 d 11 b

Acknowledgments

The publisher would like to thank the following:

Susan McKeever for assessing the manuscript. Stewart Wild for proofreading, Philip Parker for 2020 consultant review, Harish Aggarwal and Priyanka Sharma for the jacket

The publisher would like to thank the following for their kind permission to reproduce their photographs:

Key: a-above; b-below/bottom; c-center; f-far; l-left; r-right; t-top

The Trustees of the British Museum: 33cb. DK Images: British Museum 13cra, 24br, cr, fcr, 26cl, 27cl, 34tl, 37br, 45clb; Cairo Museum 21tc, 38bc; Jeremy Hunt - modelmaker 40cra; Natural History Museum, London cb; Stephen Oliver 34cl; Rosicrucian Egyptian Museum, San Jose Calif. 28c; Science Museum, London 3cr, 36cl. FLPA: Jurgen & Christine Sohns 37crb (gazelle).

imagequestmarine.com: Johnny Jensen 37cl. naturepl.com: David Kjaer clb (bird).

All other images © Dorling Kindersley
For further information see:
www.dkimages.com

FAMOUS EGYPTIAN RULERS

NAME	DJOSER	SNEFERU	KHUFU
FAMOUS FOR	Built the step pyramid at Saqqara	Built the Meidum, Bent, and Red Pyramids	Built the Great Pyramid at Giza
FAMILY	Several wives, at least one child	At least four wives and twelve children	At least four wives and nine children
DYNASTY	3rd	4th	4th
DATES	2667–2648 bce	2613–2589 bce	2589–2566 bce

NAME	KHAFRE	PEPY II	TUTHMOSIS I
FAMOUS FOR	Built the Second Pyramid at Giza, and possibly the Sphinx	Reigned longer than any other pharaoh	Was a general before marrying a princess and becoming pharaoh
FAMILY	At least four wives and fourteen children	At least four wives and one child	At least two wives and five children
DYNASTY	4th	6th	18th
DATES	2558–2532 bce	2278–2184 bce	1504–1492 bce

NAME	TUTHMOSIS III	QUEEN HATSHEPSUT	AKHENATEN
FAMOUS FOR	Conquered territory, coruled with Queen Hatshepsut as a child	Powerful female pharaoh	Reformed Egypt's religion
FAMILY	At least four wives and ten children	Two husbands (Tuthmosis II & Tuthmosis III), two children	At least four wives and nine children
DYNASTY	18th	18th	18th
DATES	1479–1425 bce	1473–1458 bce	1353–1336 bce

NAME	TUTANKHAMUN	RAMSES II	CLEOPATRA VII
FAMOUS FOR	Boy king whose tomb and treasure were found intact	Warrior king and great temple builder	Loved Julius Caesar and Mark Antony; last pharaoh
FAMILY	One wife, no surviving children	Eight major wives, more than 100 children	Four husbands, four children
DYNASTY	18th	19th	Ptolemaic
DATES	1333–1323 bce	1279–1213 bce	51–30 bce

FAMOUS EGYPTIAN GODS

NAME	RE	KHEPRI	SEKHMET
ROLE	SUN GOD; LATER KING OF THE GODS AS AMUN	CREATOR-GOD, ROLLED THE SUN DISK ACROSS THE SKY	GODDESS OF WAR
SYMBOL	SUN DISK	SCARAB BEETLE	LIONESS
CULT CENTER	HELIOPOLIS	HELIOPOLIS	MEMPHIS
ERA	FROM 2ND DYNASTY	FROM 5TH DYNASTY	FROM OLD KINGDOM

NAME	OSIRIS	ISIS	THOTH
ROLE	GOD OF THE DEAD / THE AFTERLIFE	GODDESS OF WIVES AND MOTHERS	GOD OF KNOWLEDGE AND WRITING
SYMBOL	DJED PILLAR; SHOWN AS MUMMY	GIRDLE OF ISIS; HEADDRESS WITH THRONE OR COW'S HORNS	IBIS, ALSO BABOON
CULT CENTER	ABYDOS	PHILAE	HERMOPOLIS
ERA	FROM OLD KINGDOM	FROM 5TH DYNASTY	FROM OLD KINGDOM

NAME	HORUS	ANUBIS	KHNUM
ROLE	SKY GOD	GOD OF DEAD AND EMBALMING	GOD OF NILE, ESPECIALLY CATARACTS
SYMBOL	FALCON	JACKAL	RAM
CULT CENTER	NEKHEN	CYNOPOLIS	ELEPHANTINE
ERA	FROM EARLY DYNASTIC	FROM EARLY OLD KINGDOM	FROM EARLY DYNASTIC

NAME	HATHOR	BASTET	PTAH
ROLE	GODDESS OF FERTILITY, CHILDHOOD, AND MUSIC	PROTECTED THE PHARAOH AND HELPED CROPS RIPEN	CREATOR GOD, PATRON OF CRAFTSMEN
SYMBOL	COW	LIONESS, CAT	DJED PILLAR
CULT CENTER	DENDERA	BUBASTIS	MEMPHIS
ERA	FROM 2ND DYNASTY	FROM 2ND DYNASTY	FROM PREDYNASTIC